THE ESTATE TAX
AND POLITICS

THE ESTATE TAX AND POLITICS

Walter F. Picca

iUniverse, Inc.
New York Lincoln Shanghai

The Estate Tax and Politics

iUniverse books may be ordered through booksellers or by contacting:

iUniverse
2021 Pine Lake Road, Suite 100
Lincoln, NE 68512
www.iuniverse.com
1-800-Authors (1-800-288-4677)

The information, ideas, and suggestions in this book are not intended to render legal advice. Before following any suggestions contained in this book, you should consult your personal attorney. Neither the author nor the publisher shall be liable or responsible for any loss or damage allegedly arising as a consequence of your use or application of any information or suggestions in this book.

ISBN-13: 978-0-595-42189-3 (pbk)
ISBN-13: 978-0-595-86527-7 (ebk)
ISBN-10: 0-595-42189-X (pbk)
ISBN-10: 0-595-86527-5 (ebk)

Printed in the United States of America

CONTENTS

CHAPTER 1

The Origin and Changes of the Estate Tax Explained

The principle of the estate tax goes back to the Bible: Genesis: 4:9—when Cain asked: "Am I my brother's keeper? Well, the answer—is yes. Otherwise, it is every man for himself.

Thomas Paine—proposed an inheritance tax for England—in 1791 and his pamphlet—"Common Sense" helped forge the American Revolution.

It was a break from the model of the European monarchies—divided into two main classes: the peasants and nobility—to a government dedicated to liberty and justice—elected political power (rather than hereditary) and certain human rights.

But, the ugly head—of the rich man—poor man—scenario reemerged—during the industrial revolution and into the early 20th century (under unbridled capitalism), which produced some very rich men: Astor, Carnegie, Rockefeller, Morgan, Frick, Vanderbilt, Gould, Hill, etc. The profits (capital) went into the hands of a few and there was no income or estate tax. But, the workers did not do so well. Frankly, they were exploited: long hours, low pay, dangerous working conditions, no benefits, etc. There was no justice. This by analogy is the killing of Abel. His blood cried from the ground. That led to unions. By 1912, the top 1 percent owned 56.4 percent of the wealth.

Supreme Court Justice Louis Brandeis said a century ago, "We can have concentrated wealth in the hands of a few or we can have democracy. But we cannot have both."

Thomas Jefferson provided the basic model for our estate tax in this statement:

"The descent of property of every kind therefore to all children, or to all the brothers and sisters, or other relations in equal degree, is politic measure, and a practicable one. Another means of silently lessening the inequality of property is to exempt all from taxation below a certain point, and to tax the higher portions of property in geometrical progression as they rise."

The history of the estate tax is almost parallel to the income tax. It had an on-and-off, wobbly beginning. **Theodore Roosevelt** proposed an estate tax in a message to Congress 1907, he said:

"A heavy progressive tax upon a very large fortune is in no way such a tax upon thrift or industry as a like tax would be on a small fortune. No advantage comes either to the country as a whole or to the individuals inheriting the money by permitting the transmission in their entirely of the enormous fortunes which would be affected by such a tax would help to preserve a measurable equity of opportunity for the people of the generation growing to manhood."

His proposal was not adopted until the Woodrow Wilson term of office.

The **Revenue Act of 1916** prescribed a rate schedule ranging from 1 percent on estates of less than $50,000, to 10 percent on estates over $5 million. Since then, has become a permanent source of revenue for the Federal government

In 1917, the Revenue Act raised the estate tax maximum rate to 25% and in 1924 to 40 percent.

Franklin D. Roosevelt, in a message to Congress in 1935, said:

"Wealth in the modern world does not come merely from individual effort; it results from a combination of individual effort and of the manifold uses to which the community puts that effort. The individual does not create the product of his industry with his own hands; he utilizes the many processes and forces of mass production to meet the demands of a national and international market.

And he said: "My first proposal, in line with this broad policy, has to do with inheritances and gifts. The transmission from generation to generation of vast fortunes by will, inheritance, or gifts is not consistent with the ideals and sentiments of the American people."

And he urged this wise policy of former President Theodore Roosevelt be continued and said: "I recommend, therefore, that in addition to the present estate taxes, there should be levied an inheritance, succession, and legacy tax in respect to all very large accounts received by any one legatee or beneficiary; and to prevent, so far as possible, evasions of the tax, I recommend further the imposition of gift taxes suited to this end."

And he stated the purpose: "Because of the basis on which this proposed tax is to be levied and also because of the very sound policy of encouraging a wider distribution of wealth, I strongly urge that the proceeds of this tax should be specifically segregated and applied, as they accrue, to the reduction of the national debt. By so doing, we shall progressively lighten the tax burden of the average taxpayer, and, incidentally, assist in our approach to a balanced budget."

The Revenue Act of 1932: raised the estate tax from 20% to 45% during the Great Depression. FDR raised it again in 1934 to 60% and 1935 to 70% to fund social programs and create jobs.

In 1941—FDR raised the estate tax to 77 percent—at the beginning of World War II.

The unemployment rate dropped from 23.6% in 1932 to 1.2 percent in 1944.

That is opposite—what politicians argue today: the repeal of the estate tax will spur the economy and create jobs.

From 1942 to 1976—the basic provisions remain substantially the same. The law allowed a $60,000 estate tax exemption with a tax rate ranging from 3% to 77. The gift tax came about, because gifts were made to avoid the estate tax. The Tax Reform Act of 1976: united the gift and estate tax into a single structure— and raised the exemption to $120,667. The new unified tax rates ranged from 18 percent to 70 percent.

During the Reagan presidency: the rates were changed. In 1982: the estate exemption was increased to $225,000 and the top rate of 70% on transfers of in excess of $5,000,0000 was deleted, and in 1983: the top rate of 65% on transfers of over $4,000,000 was deleted. In 1984: the top rate was reduced to 55% and the exemption increased to $325,000. The Tax Reform Act of 1986 increased the exemption to $600,000.

The Taxpayer Relief Act of 1997 raises the exemption to $1 million (phased in between 1998 to 2006). I wanted to know how it was computed. So I went to the library. There a librarian led me to The Federal Estate and Gift Tax Reporter—that explains the Unified Transfer tax of the Estate tax. It says:

The estate tax liability is determined by applying the unified rate schedule to the cumulated transfers and subtracting the gift taxes payable. The cumulated transfers to which the tentative tax applies I the sum of (1) the amount of the taxable estate and (2) the amount of the taxable gifts made by the decedent after 1976, other than gifts includible in the gross estate. Gift taxes to be subtracted in computing the estate tax included the aggregate gift tax payable on gifts made after December 31, 1976. For this purpose, the amount of gift taxes paid by a decedent after 1976 is to be determined as if the rate schedule in effect in the year of death was in effect the year of the gift. However, with respect to certain gifts subsequently included a decedent's gross estate, a credit is allowed (Code Sec. 2012) for all gift taxes paid on pre-1977 gifts.

This is legalese—written to keep people from figure things out—or blind-folded. The devil is hidden between the lines, in the sections, sub-paragraphs, and small print.

In 2000—the personal exemption was $675,000 and the top tax rate 55%. Lifetime transfers and transfers made at death are accumulated for gift and estate tax purpose. In other words: if, you can make gifts during your lifetime—i.e., dis-perse your estate (i.e., tax free) to a point. This will lower the value of your estate—and consequently your estate tax. Above—a certain point: that will be deducted from your personal exemption.

The **gift tax** was enacted in 1924 to prevent avoidance of the estate tax—and repealed in 1926. It was reinstated in 1932: the maximum rate 33 1/3% and the annual exclusion $5,000. In 1941: the gift tax rates changed to 75% of the estate tax, and in 1942: the annual exclusion was lowered to $3,000. In 1981: Reagan raised the annual gift tax exclusion to $10,000. In 2002—it was increased to $11,000, as a result of periodic inflation adjustments—and increased again in 2006—to $12,000.

In 1942, The Revenue Act set the lifetime gift tax exemption at $30,000. The law was changed in 1976: the exemption became a unified credit. That increased along with increases in the estate tax exemption. In 2002: the law set the lifetime cumulative gift exemption at $1 million. This allows the donor to exceed the per donee annual exclusion—without paying a gift tax an extra $1 million during life. However, these gifts above the annual exclusion—reduce the individual's estate tax exemption.

Bill Clinton—vetoed the HR 8—Death tax Elimination of Act—of 2000 passed by the House and Senate. There is nothing—the super-rich wanted more, than kill the estate tax. By the late 1990s, there were an estimated forty thousand households with more than $25 million and five thousand with over $100 mil-lion. And today: 18 households have a combined wealth of $185 billion.

When, George W. Bush came to office—more changes (reductions) were made in the Estate Tax—the transfer of accumulated wealth at death—to heirs. These changes are part of *The Economic Growth and Tax Relief Reconciliation Act of 2001*. He stepped on Clinton's pre-2001 law and immediately raised the exemption from $675 to $1 million in 2002, $1.5 million in 2004, $2 million in 2006, and $3.5 million in 2009—and the top tax rate was reduced from 55 percent to 45 % in stages from 2001 to 2009 and in 2010, the estate tax was repealed—for one year. These reductions and one-year elimination of the estate tax—shows the power of concentrated wealth: to manipulate lawmakers. It marks the return of the plutocrats to power. These estate tax cuts are contrary to the will of the majority of people. These are unfair tax breaks for millionaires and billionaires: between 1983 and 1998, almost all the growth in wealth of the economic boom went to the top 20 percent of household. Why not give a one-year income tax-break to the bottom twenty percent: that suffered a decline in wealth power during the same period. The purpose of this one-year repeal—was to set the stage for a permanent repeal of the estate tax. The Bush 2001 tax cuts were supposed to create surpluses for the next decade. But, reality set in: September 11th, the decline of the stock market, the war in Afghanistan and Iraq, Katrina, etc. Instead of surpluses—there were record-breaking deficits. Bush refused to reassess the tax cuts and argued, because of a the slight increase of tax revenues in 2005—his tax critics were wrong—and continued to push for the permanent repeal of the estate tax.

Six times during his presidency: the super-rich were able, through lobbyists, political donations, etc., to bring repeal of the estate tax—to vote in the House. I bet the average taxpayer: does not know what these are: HR 8, HR 2431, HR 2143, HR 586, HR 57/HR 8, HR 2610, HR 5970, HR 5638, etc. They are different bills designed to end (or reduce) the estate tax.

CHAPTER 2
4-A-Org.   4-C-Org.
4-A-men   4-C-men

FOUR CAIN ORGANICATIONS

The Policy and Taxation Group, according to their website: "Americans want the elimination of the death tax." According to new national poll: 57% prefer to keep the estate tax—and more would agree—if, there were informed.

They concluded: "The Estate Tax is unfair. It tells every American that no matter how hard you work or how wisely your manage your affairs, in the end the Federal Government is going to step in and take it way."

This is pitiful!

But, not exactly true: fewer than 1% of all estates currently are subject to the estate tax. It is fair, because, what better place to look for money—to pay the cost of government, than the great sums of assets left behind by a dead man. He has no use for it in the next world. Is it fairer; than, to tax the wages of a living man, who needs it. Somebody has to pay for government

DeathTax.com.—states in bold print: **The "Death" Tax is killing family business.** It further states:

"A family-owned business stands to lose nearly half of all its assets when it passes from one generation to the next. That's over half of everything. Including land, buildings, equipment, money, and more—all because of the current Estate Tax law which is really a tax on death."*

Heritage Foundation: the article by the William W. Beach, the director: **Now is (Still) Time to Permanently Repeal Federal Death Taxes**—has been a top priority of the GOP, since it has controlled the congress. He concludes: "Now is the time to bring this sorry chapter in U.S. tax policy to a close." This anti-estate tax article is based on pseudo-economics. It estimates: the federal estate tax is responsible alone for the loss of between 170,000 and 250,000 potential jobs each year.

OPASTCO: Repeatedly—in 2001, 2002, 22003, 2004, 2005, sent letters to members of congress: urging action on permanent death tax repeal. Here is one letter to Representative Hulshof:

excerpt

"For family-owned businesses, the projected reinstatement of the death tax following the sunset of the *Economic Growth and Tax Relief Reconciliation Act of 2001* further complicates federal estate tax planning. Families must plan for the death tax bill not knowing whether the current tax law will sunset in 2010 or Congress will enact separate legislation to extend this law. The solution to this dilemma is for Congress to finish the work it started with H.R. 1836 and pass your legislation this year."

Four Abel organizations

Citizens of Tax Justice: Citizens for Tax Justice congratulates the U.S. Senate on its decision to reject to hand a new $62 billion a year estate tax break to a small group of America's wealthiest families. A sufficient minority of Senators has said: "no" to another expensive debt.

Center on Budget and Policy Priorities:
Myth 2: The estate tax forces estates to turn over half of their assets to the government.
Reality: The few estates that pay any estate tax at all generally pay less that 20 percent of the value of their estate in taxes.

---

* **This Website was created and maintained by the Seattle Times Company.**

Americans for a fair Estate Tax: "We need fiscal responsibility from our government, not another tax break for millionaires. Currently, the estate tax only taxes estates worth more than $1.5 million ($3 million for married couples)—less than 2 percent of Americans pay any of this tax—and the first million and a half is tax-free!

Eliminating this tax will cost around $970 *billion* in lost federal government revenue over the first ten years of full repeal, and will benefit only a very small fraction of the wealthiest individuals in the country"

Responsible Wealth, a project of United for a Fair Economy, states: "We believe that permanent repeal of the estate tax would be bad for our democracy, our economy, and our society. Repealing the estate tax, a constructive part of our tax structure for 85 years, would leave an unfortunate legacy for American's future generation."

Four Cain men

Oprah Winfrey—according to Forbes—one of 400 richest Americans—said: "It is irritating that once I die, 55% of my money goes to the US government. You know why that's irritating? Because you would have already paid nearly 50%.

My reply: her success: is due more to the Television Broadcasting Network: thousands of technicians, engineers, programmers, make-up artist, and workers, than her talent. And how much of her wealth is capital gains, which she has never paid taxes on. Therefore, it is not unreasonable to divide half—between the common good—and her heirs. If, it weren't for the US government: she might be living in Africa—poor, have six kids, be infected with AIDS, and have no security (or rights).

Gregory Mankiw, Bush's former Chairman of the Council of Economic Advisers, said: "The estate is in essence a tax on capital accumulation. And as such it impedes investment and growth in productivity and living standards."

The tax is after death—not during life and like weight on a horse, it can bear some burden—or it no use to society.

George W. Bush on the campaign trail in Iowa, said in 2000: "To keep farms in the family, we are going to get rid of the death tax."

That is baloney: studies have been made since then—and no valid examples have been found—where this has happen. Although—some claim horror stories (in the past): changes should be made—not repealed.

Senator Bill Frist: "I rise today in opposition to the cruelest and most unfair tax our government imposes ... the death tax."

Answer: what is unfair: about dividing a dead man's estate: between the common good—and his heirs.

Four Abel men

William H. Gates, Sr.: "The estate tax should be regarded as just paying back to the country for all the wonderful things its made possible for the people who have that wealth."

Warren Buffet: "We have come closer to a true meritocracy than anywhere else around the world," he said. "You have mobility so people with talents can be put to the best use. Without the estate tax, you in effect will have an aristocracy of wealth, which means you pass down the ability to command the resources of the nation based on heredity rather than merit"

Paul Newman: "For those of us lucky enough to be born in this country and to have flourished here, the estate tax is a reasonable and appropriate way to return something to the common good. I'm proud to be among those supporting preservation of this tax, which is <u>one of the fairest we have.</u>"

Sheldon Cohen, former Commissioner of the IRS: "The estate tax has been with us for 90 years, brings in fairly large amounts of revenue at fairly low cost, and affects less than one-third of one percent of the population

CHAPTER 3

HOUSE OF REPRESENTIVES

House passed bill H.R. 8—making the repeal of the estate tax permanent—in April 13, 2005—by a vote of 272-162. The House bill is sponsored by Hulshof. Here are some excerpts from the congressional debate.

Six yeas (for repeal)

(R-CA-2)

Mr. Herger. Mr. Speaker, I rise in strong support of legislation to bury the destructive death tax once and for all; and I might mention that my personal experiences, even with my own family and others, has been just the opposite of the gentleman who just spoke before.

Nearly everywhere I go throughout my largely rural, agricultural district in northern California, I hear from businessmen and businesswomen and many farmers and ranchers who have had to liquidate and sell a family business or farm just to pay the Federal estate tax. This is simply wrong.

(R-IL-4)

Mr. Hastert. Mr. Speaker, we come to the floor today to address an issue of tax fairness. You see, no matter what kind of spin our friends on the other side of the aisle try to use—the death tax simply isn't fair. It's an unfair burden that the government has placed on families and small business owners. I've called it a cancer—because it's slowly destroying family farms and businesses across the nation.

(R-FL-15)

Mr. Weldon. Mr. Speaker, I want to express my strong support for H.R. 8, the Death Tax Repeal Permanency Act of 2005. I have supported this measure in the past and have introduced similar legislation to make the death tax repeal permanent. I believe it is important that we accomplished the goal of passing this in the House and the Senate and seeing that bill enacted into law.

The Death Tax needs to die. Along with the marriage penalty, the death tax is perhaps the most disgraceful tax levied by the Federal Government and it should be repealed immediately. The death tax is double taxation. Small businesses and family farmers pay taxes throughout their lifetime, then at the time of death they are assessed another tax on the value of the property on which they have already paid taxes. This is unfair, unjust and an inefficient burden on our economy.

(R-FL-22)

Mr. Shaw. I am in favor of the Hulshof bill to repeal the death tax simply because it is the right thing to do. The death tax is wrong. To go in and tax almost half of someone's estate because they have accumulated a lot and to make death an incident of taxation is wrong. It is a wrong tax, and I cannot imagine any body getting up and justifying it, other than the fact it is a revenue stream to the Federal Government, but it is the wrong one.

(R-VA-7)

Mr. Cantor. Mr. Speaker, I rise today in support of the permanent repeal of the death tax. To put it simply, the death tax is just wrong. It is wrong to encourage people to work hard all their life, only to have the government reap the benefits when they die. It is wrong to levy hefty taxes against families of thriving small business owners just because their parents were successful. It is wrong to stifle economic growth by forcing small businesses to close because of an overbearing tax bill delivered by a greedy Uncle Sam.

(R-NY-24)

Mr. Boehlert. Mr. Speaker, I rise in strong support of H.R. 8, legislation that would permanently repeal the Death Tax, a tax that haunts millions of small business owners and framers nationwide. The last thing the federal government should be doing is taking more money from small business owners and framers, and curtaining further economic growth. They are the backbone that drives our economy forward. I commend Mr. **HULSHOF** for his leadership on this issue and praise his vision to continue lowering the federal tax burden.

Six nays (against repeal)

(D-NC-21)

Mr. Etheridge. Mr. Speaker, I rise today voice my opposition to H.R. 8. As a part-time farmer and former small business owner, I have long supported responsible legislation to provide estate tax relief for family-owned businesses. Unfortunately, this bill will not accomplish that goal.

Throughout my service in the U.S. House, I have been a strong supporter of estate tax relief for family farmers and small business owners. The first bill I introduced as a Member of Congress was a bill to raise the inheritance tax exemption from $600,000 to $1.5 million and for the first time indexed it to inflation. But H.R. 8 is an extremely irresponsible bill that will add billions to our national debt for our children and grandchildren and will harm more taxpayers than it helps.

(D-CA-13)

Mr. Stark. Mr. Speaker, I guess it becomes my job to point out that the Republicans are at it gain. Another huge tax cut or break for less than 1 percent of the richest Americans while they turn their back and cut Medicaid, refuse to recognize that Social Security is not in crisis but needs some adjustment, cut Head Start, cut programs for housing, cut programs for the environment, fail to provide the promised benefits to our 140,000 servicemen in Iraq, turn their back on all that is American to give a few dollars to the very richest of Americans.

(D-CA-8)

Ms. Pelosi. "Mr. Speaker, in the 20th century, in the early part of the 20th century, our country made a decision to honor our American value of fairness by moving forward toward a progressive system of taxation. But under 10 years of Republican tax rule, this Congress has consistently passed legislation that has moved away from a progressive Tax Code. Republican tax policies have rewarded wealth over work. In its analysis of the President's budget, the nonpartisan Congressional Budget Office found that tax rate on wage income is nearly twice the rate of capital income, unearned. And now today Republicans have come to the floor with an estate bill continuing their harmful approach.

(D-TX-25)

Mr. Doggett. "Mr. Speaker, I rise in opposition to this latest Republican assault on Social Security and on fiscal sanity. At a time of apparently unending war and the largest budget deficits in American history, our Republican colleagues are intent on solving a crisis that does not exist.

As the President wastes millions of our taxpayer dollars crisscrossing this country to declare that there is no Social Security trust fund and questioning the full faith and credit of the Federal Government, his Republican allies here seem intent on actually making his dire and inaccurate statements a self-fulfilling prophecy. Today, what they propose is to borrow from the Social Security trust fund and to borrow from the Medicare trust fund in order to give more tax breaks to the richest one-tenth of 1 percent of the people of this country.

(D-WA-7)

Mr. McDermott. Mr. Speaker, my colleague from Florida, I wish he would stay, because we are here today because the Republican majority would like to repeal the estate tax, but they have forgotten history.

I am sure my colleague was not here, but I would like to remind him that it was a Republican, President, Teddy Roosevelt, who strongly supported an estate tax in the first place. Here is what he said:

"The man of great wealth," Teddy said, "owes a particular obligation to the State because he derives special advantages from the mere existence of government."

(D-IL-5)

MR. Emanuel. Mr. Speaker, I rise in opposition to HR 8, which continues, in my view, the polices by the majority of three tax cuts, in 4 years, with four straight record-breaking deficits that have added $2 trillion in 4 years to the Nation's debt. And here again the majority offers $850 million of tax cuts to the wealthiest families in this country.

When you get in a hole that is $2 trillion deep, rule one, stop digging. If you cannot figure that out, you cannot produce any more when it comes to economic growth for this country or jobs or resolving the health care crisis of the educational crisis we have in the country. My view is repeating the same mistake and expecting a different result is a sign that you have lost your bearing.

CHAPTER 4

☺ ☺ ☺ ☺ ☺ ☺ ● ● ● ● ● ●

THE SENATE

On—June 8, 2006: The Senate fell short of the 60 votes needed to override a filibuster threat by Democrats—to invoke cloture on H.R. 8, to make the repeal of the estate tax permanent—by a vote of 57 to 41. The bill was sponsored by senator Jon Kyl.

Excerpts from the congressional debate
Six nays (against repeal)
(D-IL)

Mr. Durbin. Mr. President, we are now considering the repeal of the estate tax. The estate tax is a tax paid by 2 out of every 1,000 Americans. It is not a tax that will affect the vast majority of Americans because they have not accumulated wealth in their lifetime to be subject to the tax.

The New York Times went to the Farm Bureau and asked them: Name for us a single example of a family being force to sell its farm because of estate tax liability. Not one single example derived from the American Farm Bureau. They couldn't find one. I did the same thing in Illinois. Not one farm has been lost because of Federal estate tax liability.

(D-CA)

Ms. Feinstein: Madam President, I rise to oppose this bill. With an $8.4 trillion national debt, a budget deficit that will exceed $300 billion this year, a looming entitlement crisis, and a mounting alternative minimum tax problem, full repeal of the estate tax at this time is simply not responsible.

We have until 2010 to make decisions about the estate tax. In doing so, time will afford us the opportunity to make more informed choices, with a more complete picture of our Nation's fiscal health.

(D-MA)

Mr. Kerry. Madam President, today we are debating repeal of the estate tax. Many of us have supported reform to the estate tax in a reasonable way that will help families keep their small businesses and farms. But this debate about repeal of the estate tax has become unreasonable and fiscally irresponsible.

Some in the Republican majority are calling for full and permanent repeal of the estate tax and have referred to the estate tax as "immoral" and "vicious" I disagree. Only very wealthy Americans will benefit from the proposal before us today. It is a proposal that does not reward work, entrepreneurship, or innovation.

(D-MI)

Mr. Levin. Madam President, this bill to repeal the estate tax is unfair and unaffordable. Full repeal is estimated by the Joint Committee on Taxation to cost $776 billion over the first 10 years it is in full effect. And in fact that cost would be nearly $1 trillion when the interest on the extra debt that would be required are taken into account.

Repealing the estate tax would only benefit a tiny percentage of the very wealthiest Americans among us by enabling them to pass additional millions of dollars to their heirs tax-free. It would shift an even larger share of the Nation's tax burden and debt onto the backs of average working families and our children and grandchildren.

(D-IA)

Mr. Harkin. Madam President, I am dumfounded that the Senate is debating yet another gigantic tax break for the wealthiest people in our society. The Republicans are pushing this latest giveaway despite that fact that we are facing a deficit, this year, in excess of $300 billion a year, despite the fact that they have run up $2 trillion in new debt since President Bush took office, despite the fact they have increased spending by 25 percent in just 5 years time, and despite the fact that we are spending $10 billion a month on seemingly endless wars in Iraq and Afghanistan.

The level of irresponsibility is just breathtaking. This is a tax break we cannot afford, benefiting people who don't need it. Currently, the estate tax impacts far less than 1 percent of the wealthiest families in American. And you can be sure that these are not families facing economic hardship or struggling to make ends meet.

(D-MA)

Mr. Kennedy. Mr. President, the audacity of the Bush administration and their congressional allies truly knows no limit. In spite of all of the urgent problems facing our Nation—from the ongoing war in Iraq, to the devastating hurricane damage along the gulf coast that has not been yet been repaired, to the outrageously high gasoline prices that are squeezing American families—the top Republican priority is eliminating the estate tax for the richest families in the country. President Bush's policies have already added nearly $3 trillion to the national debt in the last 5 years. Now, they are proposing more of the same, more tax breaks benefiting only the wealthiest among us.

Six yeas (for repeal)
(R-AZ)

Mr. Kyl. Mr. President, we are going to have an opportunity very shortly to do something historic; that is, to begin consideration of a process by which we can either eliminate or substantially reduce the impact of the most unfair tax of all, the estate tax, on small business, on family farms, on Americans of all stripes who worry that they will have to pay up to half of what they have put into their life savings, their business, their farm, to the Government in an estate tax.

It has been found by Gallup surveys and others that the American people believe this is the most unfair tax and by percentages, 60 to 70 percent agree that it should be eliminated. To some extent there has been an argument that I have to address because it is a straw man. That argument is that this is all about helping the most wealthy families. That is not correct.

(R-AL)

Mr. Shelby. Mr. President, I rise today to voice my strong and unwavering support for a full repeal of the estate tax, or the death tax, as we often refer to it.

Until World War I, the Government only imposed an estate tax or inheritance tax to raise revenue to fund expenses directly related to the necessities of war.

Even then, the rate was measured. However, that practice changed after Word War I, and unlike four previous occasions, the tax was not repealed once a peace agreement was reached. In fact, the tax continued to increase until it reached 70 during Franklin Roosevelt's administration.

What was once a means to finance war eventually became a significant revenue stream that funded aspects of a growing Federal bureaucracy. Today, the estate tax continues to provide a significant revenue stream to the Federal coffers and functions as a redistribution of personal wealth and punishment, basically, to those successful business owners seeking a better way of life.

(R-KY)

Mr. Bunning. Mr. President, I rise today in strong favor of abolishing one of the unjustified taxes we have in America today: the death tax. American should not have to talk to their undertaker and their tax man on the same day. Small businesses and family farms should not be forced to close down in order to pay the Government money because a loved one has passed away. Unfortunately, I see this happening when I travel back to Kentucky every week. We are not looking out for our economy or our very own people when we change them for inheriting the American dream.

The mom and pop diner on the corner of our down squares and third-generation farms in our rural areas are being unduly burdened by a repressive Tax Code. In fact, many are forced to close their doors or sell out, just so they can afford what the Government says they owe.

(R-CO)

Mr. Allard. Mr. President, I rise to offer my strong support for permanent repeal of the death tax.

It is said that "a penny saved is a penny earned". Unfortunately, that is not the case for many Americans—especially those who have family business and farms. Instead of being rewarded for their initiative and determination, entrepreneurs are penalized for taking advantage of all this country has to offer.

For much of the 21st century, the death tax has burdened this country's hardest working citizens. It is finally time for Congress to permanently repeal this unfair tax. That is why I am pleased to support the Death Tax Repeal Permanency Act. Death should not be a taxable event.

(R-MO)

Mr. Bond. Madam President, 5 years ago Congress took steps to end the death tax. Now the American people expect us to finish the job.

We need to end permanently the tax that punishes American values of savings and investment and of building small businesses and family farms and ranches.

The death tax punishes the American dream—making it virtually impossible for the average American family to build wealth across generations.

The death tax is anti-savings, anti-family, and anti-investment. It is quite simply—un-American.

(R-TN)

Mr. Bill Frist. In a few moments we will have a vote on cloture on the motion to proceed to H.R. 8, and we need to be very clear about what this vote means. A vote in favor is a vote to move forward with this important debate. A vote against is a vote to kill any change of repealing or even reforming this onerous tax and is a vote in favor of returning the death tax to the pre-2001 confiscatory rate of 55 percent, an exemption of only $1 million per person.

Back in 2001, we passed a gradual phase out of the death tax—real progress. Under that 2001 Economic Growth Tax Relief and Reconciliation Act, the death is scheduled to disappear in 2010.

But under the terms of this compromise legislation, after 2010 it comes roaring back with that tax level of 55 percent in 2011. That is why we need to act. We need a permanent fix, and that is what this vote is all about.

CHAPTER 5

COMMENTARY

Those saying the estate tax is unfair—is extreme egoism. Think about it: who contributes most to wealth building: the government and society or heirs. Mr. Bond: the estate tax: "is un-American". Both capitalism and the estate tax are an American principle: the strong and weak force gone amuck in the House.

Calling the estate tax—a Death Tax—is misleading, in that it is not a tax on death—itself, rather than, a tax on large sums of accumulated wealth—transferred to heirs—when a person dies.

Many congressmen—say the estate tax is unfair; but, heirs do not pay the inheritance tax—on assets of an estate—that pays the estate tax: that is fair. Without the estate tax—all assets of the deceased are transferred tax-free, which creates super-affluent families.

The estate tax—returns some to the general welfare—rather than all to heirs—or beneficiaries: that is fair.

The main complaint—by the supporters of HR 8: the estate tax destroys family farms and businesses. But, what has happen in the past—is not valid today, because the exemptions, rates, and rules have been changed. The percentage of estates subject to the tax in 2004: that were family farms and businesses—2%.

Mr. Levin says: "One-third of the estate tax is paid by the wealthiest one of one thousand Americans. I think that is one-tenth of 1 percent. Not farmers or small business people. That is the lamest argument brought to this floor in recent memory."

Don't blame the failure of families farms and businesses in the second and third generation—on the estate tax—when other reasons—are more likely to blame.

Criticisms of the estate tax in the House and Senate debate are largely, based on out-of-date information, twisting the facts, and misinformation.

Mr. Bunning went as far to say: the estate tax—destroys mom and pop stores—tearing at our heart.

This argument is a hoax. In the words of Senator Kerry: "Often it's argued that the estate tax needs to be repealed to assist small businesses. There is no concrete evidence that a family-run business has been put out of business by the estate tax. If the AMT is not addressed it will hurt many more small businesses, but instead of addressing it, Republicans prefer to promote the myth that the estate tax shatters small businesses."

If, congressmen and senators wanted to shield family farms and businesses from the estate tax, they could: by increasing the QFOBI exclusion—or exempt them, but, this is not their intention: it is used as a ploy—to repeal the estate tax on the estates of the superrich, which are not family farms and businesses.

The 1997 Taxpayer Relief Act did this in part. It provided for a qualified family owned business interest—exclusion up to $1.3 million—from the estate tax. This was Clinton's targeted therapy.

But, this did not satisfy Bush—he wants the death tax on estates of millionaires and billionaires—eliminated—using the save the family farm and business artifice.

That is HR 8—the permanent repeal of the estate tax, which is not necessary to save family farms and businesses.

EGTRRA—2001—set it up—i.e., the gradual phase-out. Let's continue with congressional debate.

Mr. Bunning also said: "Americans should not have to talk to their undertaker and their tax man on the same day". This, of course, is not literal. The standard time: nine months to pay the tax. But, under Section 6166 of the Tax Code—you can get up to 10 years to pay in installments and a deferment of the first installment up to five years, or 14 years.

"It's a myth, says **Senator Reid:** "that we need to repeal the estate tax to protect and preserve small businesses and family farms."

The statement made by Mr. Shaw—is not, exactly correct: the government will take almost half, when you die. Under the current law: 2006: the personal exemption is 2 million: double for married couples. Take for example: the net value of the estate (after deductions) is $5 million. One million is taxed at 46 percent: that is 9.2 percent of the total. The estate tax can be reduced more—by making charitable donations. That is not unfair.

The average percentage of estates paid in taxes in 2004—20 percent, far below the top rate. This is called—the effective rate. So, the statement made by Bill Frist in the congressional records: that family-owned business stand to lose nearly half of all assets—including land, buildings, equipment, money and more—is simply not factual.

Without the family farm and business—argument: there is no case for the repeal of the estate tax. Mr. Harkin said: "Neal Harl, one of the Nation's most respected lawyers and agricultural economist, knows of no instance where a farm has had to be sold because of the estate tax." "Let's be honest," said Mr. Obama, "this is not about saving small businesses and family farms."

The minerals in ground: oil, coal, iron, etc. are part of the commonwealth, but oil executive think they deserve the lion's share. For example, the total compensation of oil executives for 2004:

Name	Company	Salary, Bonuses, etc.	Value of options
Ray R. Irani	Occidental Pet.	$30.1 million	$181.3 million
Lee R. Raymond	Exxon Mobil	$27.8 million	$72.7 million
J.J. Mulva	ConocoPhillips	$6.9 million	$36 million
David J. O'Reily	Chevron Texaco	$6.3 million	$7.8 million

Bill: HR 8—the death tax repeal permanency act of 2005: allows the transfer of these large estates of accumulated wealth to heirs (or beneficiaries)—tax-free (upon death)

Mr. Allard said: death should not be a taxable event: it is not—for more than 99 percent of the people. But, the true of the matter, more should be.

Birth should not be a taxable event; but it is: every person born inherits his share of the deficit—as of October 2, 2006: $28,302 and that is growing.

Mr. Kyl—said: the American people according to Gallup Poll—favor repeal—60 to 70 percent. The date of this poll is critical. Polls taken after people have been misled—or prior to knowing the facts—are not valid. I do not believe the people knew the facts—then. Some, thought it was a tax on death.

Bill First, the Senate Majority Leader, statement is misleading also. Repeal or back to $1 million and 55 percent in 2011. The personal exemption is $1 million (double for married couples). The top rate is 55—percent—but, applies on estates valued from $3 million to $10 million. The bottom rate is 41 percent. Mortgages, auto loans, credit card debt, funeral expenses, probate costs, etc.—are deductible. What Frist and others senators and congressmen failed to mention, who used these figures, the average effective rate was 19 percent in 2001, far below the top rate. So, the picture is not near as bleak as members of congress indicated.

Bill Frist states: we have only two choices: repeal or back to 2001—in 2011. But, there is a third: **reform.**

I think 55% is a little too high; i.e., for normal times—and the jump from zero to 41%—is too abrupt. And, the estate tax would be fairer—if, the progression of rates were more gradual. But, I would not throw out the baby with the bath water. As, Warren Buffet said: repealing the estate tax—"would be a terrible mistake."

What needs to be repealed—is the repeal of the estate tax for 2010: that is the killing of Abel!

The vociferous attempt to kill the estate tax permanently—by Bill Frist—can be explained: it is estimated—the repeal will save his estate $13 million in taxes. That begs the question: who is he representing: himself and rich political donors—or the people.

And this is why the super-rich are behind the repeal—so persistently, for example, retired CEO of Exxon-Mobil: will save an estimated $146 million.

And one reason: the White House (Bush) is behind HR 8: the House Committee on Government Reform estimates that the estate tax repeal could save the heirs of President Bush, Vice president **Cheney** and 11 Cabinet members as much as $344 million.

So, when Bush was campaigning in Iowa: he was not thinking so much of farmers—he was thinking more of himself. He states on his White House website: "the greatest help for those most in need"—referring to his tax policy: that is BS. His tax cuts have been proven over and over again—they are skewed towards the wealthy—and he continues to use this false ad.

The Joint Committee on Taxation: estimates the in 2011, permanent repeal would cost $55 billion in lost revenue and in the decade after 2011, $800 billion.

The **Center on Budget and Policy Priorities** says: it will cost roughly $1 trillion from 2010 to 2021 (including $222 billion interest on the national debt).

After HR 8, the permanent repeal of the estate tax, failed in the Senate: Bill Frist led the fight to pass the bill—called the Trifecta. It was an attempt to bribe members of congress—by linking the minimum wage hike—to a drastic reduction of the estate tax on millionaires and billionaires—and extend popular tax breaks. That rightly failed—also

And there are more bills—lined up; if, one doesn't work, they will try another. After HR 8—failed in the Senate: Bush strategist Karl Rove said to a NFIB audience: "Don't look at it as a defeat. This is war, and we need to make an ongoing commitment to winning the effort to repeal the death tax." The estate tax—called by Rove—the "death tax" is a tax on the wealthiest Americans—not those in greatest need.

Those congressmen and senators—that support HR 8—are advocating the transfer of great sums of wealth from one generation to the next—tax free—creating a super-wealthy class: that don't have to work for a living: that is un-American.

Those congressmen and senator that rose in support of HR 8—are destroying one leg of the American progressive tax system: the inheritance tax: that redistributes a part of concentrated wealth; generally, from investment income (or profit from the labors of others).

Actually, the inheritance tax is more just—than, the income tax; since, it is a tax on income—which heirs have not earned. Whereas, the income tax is a tax on earned income.

The estate tax or inheritance is just, because it divides accumulated wealth between heirs and the common good.

The fact, many states, recently, repealed the inheritance tax; is a sign of the growing power of the super-rich.

It places a bigger burden on income achieve by labor—and relieves the person who has not earned it—heirs: from paying a tax. That is unfair.

Opponents of the estate tax—say it is double taxation. Not really, one is a tax on the income of the living and one is a tax on the accumulated wealth of the decedent—before it is transferred to heirs: two, distinctly, different taxes. Anyways, most things are double or triple taxed—including income.

These taxes are to pay for hundreds and thousands of government services—and benefits.

Which—one—do you want to eliminate: the Army, the courts, the schools, the police, the libraries, welfare, medical care, road building, or the sewage system. The double taxation argument is not valid. There are local, state and federal taxes.

Each principality—provides a different service: that is triple taxation.

What is the difference: one tax of 60 percent—or a 20 percent tax at the local, state, and federal level.

If, you don't tax the immense estates of the deceased, generated; mostly, from investment income (profits or capital gains)—you place more tax on labor. I have not heard one person say: the Death Tax should be 100 percent. But, on the other hand: I have heard—many say: wealth should be transfer to the next generation—100 percent tax-free.

Both—of these positions—are unjust.

Without the income and estate tax: you create a permanent American super-rich class. **Ralph Nader** said: "Democracy or avaricious plutocracy, that is the question."

The bad thing about a plutocracy—or oligarchy: it has the power to do what good for themselves and bad for the people. And that is made possible by the concentration of wealth (or capital) in the hands of a few, who buy and control the mass media, and influence (or control) lawmakers—or political parties through political donations, etc. In 1890 former President Hayes pondered: "the wrongs and evils of the money piling tendency of our country, which is changing laws, government, and morals and giving all power to the rich." And here is proof—this has taken place in American—in the last 25 years.

The reduction in the top income tax-rates

The reduction of the dividend tax to 15%

The reduction of the capital gains tax to 15%

The scheme by executives to issue themselves: stock options and grants, as compensation—thereby reducing their income tax to 15%.

The reductions in the estate tax.

The repeal of the estate tax—for 1 year.

The incessant attempts to repeal the estate tax—permanently, which they branded—the Death Tax.

HR 5638 recently passed by House reduces the estate tax to15%—beginning in 2010.

Eight-five percent for the **great man** and his heirs—and 15% for the commonwealth—is out of balance.

Warren Buffet says: "Do you know what is going on here? It is class warfare. My class is winning".

Proponents of estate tax repeal or reduction—argue—it will create jobs.

It might help—a little—or might not.

What it does—make the rich—richer.

There is no assurance—those who receive tax cuts—are going to employ more people—they might take a luxury cruise instead—or buy more real estate.

Mr. Harkin said: "Repeal of the estate tax would not create a single new job. It would do nothing to increase productivity or competitiveness. It would do nothing to improve the education of our children or the general well-being of the American people. No, this is a pure and simple giveaway—a bonanza for those who have already received the lion's share of the tax breaks passed over the last 5 years."

The absent of the inheritance tax did not prevent the depression of 1893—when, twenty percent of the workforce was unemployed and men foraged for food in garage dumps, while the rich gave lavish parties, sometimes costing $100,000.

India has no inheritance tax—over one-third of its population lives in poverty and has more than one-third of the world's blind, some of which can be prevented for less than $10—and it has 20 billionaires.

Mexico has no inheritance tax—over half the population lives in poverty—twenty percent—extreme—and it has 10 billionaires.

If, you had a choice: of allowing the rich to pay for cosmetic surgery for their dog, or buy a $500 bottle of wine for their dinner, or buy a $500,000 wrist watch—or provide health insurance for the 40 million uninsured: what could you do.

That is what it is all about: fairness.

Nobody—is advocating—soaking the rich—just what is fair: that is the American Dream (wealth).

Just, put humans before dogs.

Unfortunately—the dogs of the rich—live better—than, the children of the poor.

The former chairman of the Education and Workforce Committee is building a personal golf course from profits of student loans: Sallie paid him from 1995 to 2004: $225 million. And Bush reduced his income, dividend, capital gains, and estate taxes. That is not fair. And the Republican dominated congress, recently, eliminated the college tuition credit and increased interest on student loans— beginning July 1, 2006.

On the Jim Lehrer News Hour: I heard a journalist from the Wall Street Journal interviewed by **Ray Suarez,** say: The Bush Tax cuts were working, because of a strong economy and low unemployment rate. They are one boy with ten men pushing a bus. And Bush lightened the load—by cutting and reducing social programs. But, he is ignoring the negative effects of the record-breaking deficits. One of those: No Child Left Behind—is under funded by $40 billion. But, most of all: he is missing this factor: these tax cuts increases the flow of wealth to the top—creating a US plutocracy—a government controlled by the rich. The first thing a plutocracy does: cut taxes on the rich. Reagan did it. Forbes tried to do it. Bush has done it—in 2001, 2003, and 2006. His next goal: HR 8—or the next best thing—a big cut in the estate tax. And, the mass media has backed him—by enlarge. The rich have gotten richer by tax cuts under Reagan and Bush, and the poor—have gotten poorer by rising prices. It is taking place right before our eyes: tearing down $1 million homes and building houses with double and triple the floor space—called McMansions. While, at the same time—there is a lack of affordable low-income housing (or rentals)

In 2005: the income of the top 1 percent grew by 17 percent—3 percent by the average worker. Those making the minimum wage—have not had a wage increase in nine years. While, during the same period: the congress has voted to raise its wages eight times, nearly $28,000. Do—the super-rich—really, need tax relief—on top of enormous income and wealth gains in the last twenty-five: the Bush Administration and Congress thinks so. Less than a month after the Senate failed to repeal the estate tax, the House passed HR 5638—called: *The Permanent Estate Relief Act of 2006.* It increases the exemption and reduces the tax rate—

drastically. It is tax relief for the top less than 1%, who don't need it—and a greater tax burden for the more than 99 percent. It should be called: the labor tax burden act. Three Bush tax cuts are called tax relief acts. When it increases the deficit—it is a (double) tax burden on labor: the debt—plus the interest.

Proof—that wealth is not moving towards the bottom—4.3 million people fell below the poverty line, since Bush took office—and that was reported in back in May of 2005.

According to Professor Wolff: between 1983 and 2004—bottom 40 percent of households have seen a decline in their net worth.

Worst of all, the federal deficit has risen to $8.552 trillion, as of October 4, 2006—and is growing at the rate of $1.68 billion a day, since September 30, 2005.

Forty-five million people are without health insurance: 8 more million since Bush took office.

To compensate for tax cuts for the rich—cuts have been made in health, education, and welfare, etc.

Instead of the paid-in Social Security surplus being put in a Trust: it is spent as tax revenue. That is like—you give someone money—you trust—to hold—to keep you from spending it; instead, they make a payment on their credit card debt.

US Government is using the Enron—accounting methods—to deceive the America people.

The Federal Budget deficit—is understated for two reasons: sizeable US government expenses are off budget. And, it does not count the debt—created—by spending the Social Security Surplus—in the Federal budget.

As of October 4, 2006: $1.99 trillion is owed the Social Security Trust Fund (i.e., from FICA payroll taxes). Soon, the benefits will exceed payroll taxes and rapidly climb to $100 billion in 2015 and $500 billion in 2025.

Future generations—must make up what we misallocated (or spent)—or drastically, cut benefits. Instead, of having a fund to pay Social Security and Medicare benefits—the government must levy new taxes—to pay for what already has been paid. Do I make myself clear. You have been ripped-off.

Mr. Doggett put it this way: "It is taking from the hard-working employees and employers who are paying their Social Security money and transferring that wealth over to the richest one-tenth of 1 percent."

Bush has done this by spending these funds and cutting taxes on the super-rich. The Social Security surplus—was $86.5 billion in 2005: that was spent as tax revenue, but that debt is not included in the Federal Budget deficit.

The siphoning off of the Social Security Trust fund for other purposes has been going on for years. There is nothing left in these funds, except IOUs.

Proof—that wealth (or capital) is moving to the top: the average net worth of the nation's 400 wealthiest in 2002: $955 million: that climbed to $2.8 billion in 2005.

According to Professor Wolff: 90 percent of the increase in wealth between 1983 and 2004—has gone to the top 20 percent of households.

The repeal of the estate (or inheritance) tax—would increase the gap between the rich and poor.

Does this sound familiar: We meet in the midst of a nation brought to the verge of moral, political and material ruin. Corruption dominates the ballot box, the legislature, the Congress, and touches even the ermine of the bench. The people are demoralized … the fruits of the toil of millions are boldly stolen to build up colossal fortunes … we breed two great classes—the paupers and millionaires.

This was the preamble to the Populist Party—in 1892.

This situation—is created when—there is no income and inheritance tax.

Populist **"Sockless" Jerry Simpson** called these two extremes: "the robbed and robbers".

He said: "the allied hosts of monopolies, the money power, great trusts, and railroad corporations, who seek the enactment of laws to benefit them and impoverish the people."

Since, Reagan and Bush have taken office—we have return to the Gilded Age—a period of unprecedented wealth and corruption—as seen in the Abramoff scandal.

In 1982: there were 13 billionaires: in 2004: 374. And the inflation-adjusted value of the minimum wage is 29 percent; lower today, than it was in 1979.

Bill Frist, Senator Majority Leader, says: the most unfair part of the tax code is the estate tax. Actually, the most unfair part of the tax code is the Bush's tax cuts—which he staunchly supported. He stands behind the president at the signing of the three Bush Tax cuts—smiling.

The last one—in 2006: the extension of the reduction of the dividend and capital tax gains to 15 percent—to the year 2011. This is outrageous—considering the growing deficit. Bear in mind: 54 per cent of all capital gains and dividend income flows to the 0.2 percent of households with annual income over $1 million; only, 4 percent flows to the bottom 64%—according to the Center on Budget and Policy Priorities.

Now—he is angry—because: the estate tax repeal—failed to pass. He said: when, his mom died in 2003, it was painful for him to hand the Federal government a check for over $300,000. What he failed to mention: how much he received. He is one of the richest men in the Senate.

Senator Bill Frist said—after the repeal of the estate tax failed in the Senate:

"The Death Tax is an unfair burden inflicted upon America's small businesses, farmers, and families during a time of grieving and pain. Wiping this vicious tax from the books is a matter of principle."

He is a diehard plutocrat.

Here is what Senator Kyl said: "The U.S. Senate today missed an opportunity to support an initiative that would have provided long-needed relief to families and family-owned businesses across the country. A clear majority of the Senate represents the growing sentiment in American—that the death tax is the most unfair section of our tax code."

You see—how (some) politicians distort things. Both used the same hoax. Senator Kennedy put it this way: "These small businesses and farms are being used as a sympathetic Trojan horse to conceal those who would really benefit from the estate tax repeal. The real beneficiaries of repeal would be the heirs of the richest men and women in America."

The growing sentiment in America—is reform, not repeal.

It is one of the fairest taxes—because, it taxes: the most able, rather than the less able.

Mr. Dorgan (D-NM) said: "The wealthiest 1 percent of Americans now own a bigger piece of the pie than the poorest 90 percent. That gap is growing. This legislation will once again decide to expand the inequality of income in this country."

Do you know: every year for the last eight years: the estate tax rates have been lowered five times and the exemption increased six times by congress—and the minimum wage has stayed the same. That is doubly unfair—the growing imbalance of wealth—and the reduction (or repeal) of the estate tax.

In the United States—the gap between the rich and poor is greater than any industrialized nation in the world.

One reason: low wages at the bottom and excessive compensation at the top—no limits.

Secondly, the US income tax turns flat—at $325,000: the people earning $1 million, $5 million, or $10 million: pay the same tax rate: as those earning $325,000.

And third: the step-by-step eradication of the estate tax—which opponents call the Death Tax.

President Theodore Roosevelt said: "Most great civilized countries have an income tax and an inheritance tax."

According to Ralph Nader: "The logic of the inheritance tax is unassailable and deeply rooted in American history."

What HR 8 does—is repeal the estate tax—which is the America's form of an inheritance tax: allowing the passage of accumulated wealth—to the next generation tax free: one generation becomes rich, the next super rich, and the next super-super rich. Now, we are back to the evils of hereditary succession of economic and political power. That happens; when wealth is concentrated in the hands of few: they raise their wages and lower their taxes—and they cut social programs and freeze wages at the bottom—as done in the Bush Administration.

True—**capitalism** is the engine of goods and services (i.e., the profit motive), but, without some socialism: you have the evils of the industrial revolution and the early 20th century. FDR's New Deal—is a form of socialism.

Meizhu Lui, Executive Director of **United for a Fair Economy,** (referring to bill—HR 5970) said: "Tax cuts for the rich means still more decreases in funding for public education, student loans, small businesses and other paths to individual prosperity. A $100-per-month increase in the minimum wage won't make up for those losses for low-income people. And gutting the estate tax would contribute to the creation of a financial aristocracy, a permanent class based on inherited wealth. Don't the "conservatives" understand that goes against the intentions of the Founding Fathers."

In order to restore fiscal responsibility—all the major tax cuts of the Bush plutocracy—should be repealed. America is digging its own grave—by the rapid growing Federal budged deficit. The latest estimate for 2006: $361 billion. But, the real deficit: counting off-budget debt: $574 billion. That is the Big Deception.

From 1942 to 1977—the estate tax exemption stayed at $60,000 (i.e., for 35 years). Since, Reagan and Bush took office, there has been a rapid escalation of the personal exemption: from $161,563 in 1980 to $3.5 million in 2009—a giant leap in 29 years. It looks like this on a chart.

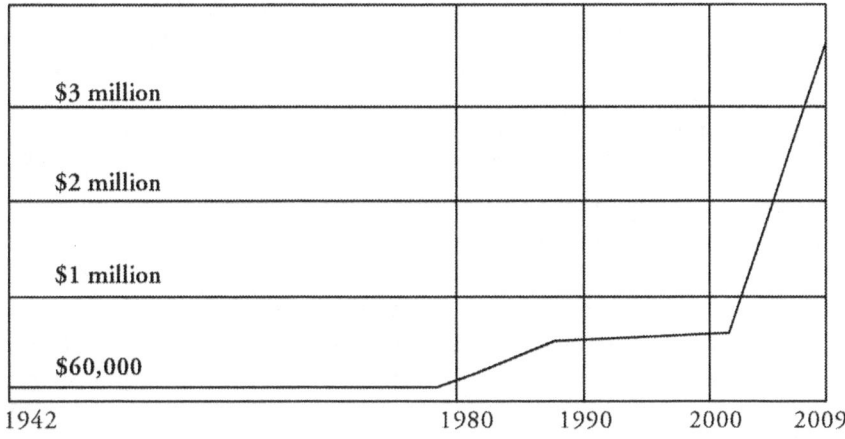

The problem with today's estate tax—it lacks progression. It is based on an old table. The personal exemption was repeatedly raised—submerging the lower marginal rates. Now, it starts at 46 percent. The rate progression should begin above the personal exemption line—not below. The first tax rate should begin at 10% or less—not 46.

The Pomeroy proposed amendment: setting the exemption at $3 million (double for couples)—beginning in 2006: is too much, exempting 99.7 percent of estates and the single 47 percent tax rate—lacks progression: it is half-way between good and bad.

S 420—the Kyl compromise is 75 percent lopsided: $8 million exemption and a 15% tax rate.

Whereas, the Hulshof-Kyl permanent repeal of the estate tax is 100 percent bad.

Allan Sloan of Newsweek said: "In the name of preserving family farms and keeping small businesses in the family, President Bush would create a new class of landed aristocrats who would inherit billions tax-free, invest the money, watch it compound tax-free, and hand it down tax-free to their heirs."

HR 5638—recently, passed in the House after HR 8 the repeal failed—is a drastic reduction of the estate tax. It raises the exemption to $5 million (double for couples) and reduces the tax rate to 15% on estates up to $25 million and 30% over $25 million.

This bill is anemic (i.e., will generate very little revenue); where, there is a great surplus. Only, 0.33 percent of estates are subject to the tax, because of the high exemption. It is plutocratic piece of legislation—without public input (debate).

It reunifies the estate and gift tax—and that increases the lifetime accumulative gift credit from $1 million to $5 million per person. These are inter vivos gifts in excess of the annual per donee exclusion. What this does: it allows the donor to transfer wealth by gift-giving during life or after death up to $5 million per person or $10 million for couples without paying a gift or estate tax. That is a double tax avoidance scheme

It also is bad, because it links the two tax rates: to the capital gains tax—like Siamese twins. These are two different taxes. The capital gains tax should be changeable—without changing the estate tax—and vice verse.

The capital gains tax should have never been lower in the first place. Capital gains are derived from capital investments. Why, should this income be taxed at a lower rate than income from labor—or business income (or profit).

This linkage is sinister: it puts pressure on congress to extend the capital gains tax cut—to prevent an increase in the estate tax: in 2011 to 20 and 40 percent.

It is a sweetheart deal for the superrich: the exemptions are indexed for inflation: the unused exemptions of one spouse—is transferable to the other. It includes a big increase in the generation skipping transfer tax exemption.

This legislation is corrupt from another standpoint: attached to the bill—a provision to create a new 60 percent deduction for qualified timber capital gains—to increase its chances of passage. It shows to what extent plutocrats will go—to drastically cut the estate tax. It borders on fraud. If, the bill won't pass on its own two feet—it is immoral to add extraneous enticements.

This bill would cost between $744 billion to $820 billion with interest over the 2012 to 2021 period, depending on, whether, the lower capital gains tax rate is extended, or not. Its passage: shows the House of Representatives no longer represent the people.

Rep. Dennis Kucinich put it this way: "H.R. 5638, the estate tax legislation, should be more accurately described as the American Idle Act, I-D-L-E, because it relieves the children of billionaires and multimillionaires of over one-quarter of a trillion dollars of estate taxes in just the five years starting in 2013. The $2,600 per taxpayer loss of revenue will take money from our schools, our health care, our senior citizens, and our veterans."

The House debate of HR 5638—took place on June 22, 2006. Here are some excerpts:

Four yeas
(R-VA-7)

Mr. Cantor. Mr. Speaker, today we are considering a bill that would move us a step closer to full repeal of the death tax, a goal which I fully support.

(R-MI-4)

Mr. Camp of Michigan. Mr. Speaker, today I rise in support of a permanent solution to the "estate tax" or what many call the "death tax". Whatever name it goes by, it is a tax on the American dream.

(R-CA-49)

Mr. Issa. I will vote for this bill today because it is the best we can do at this time. In my mind this is only a down payment, and I will work with the Congress to permanently eliminate this unreasonable and unfair double taxation.

(D-AL-5)

Mr. Cramer. Mr. Speaker. I thank the chairman for yielding me this time. I do rise in support of the Permanent Estate Tax Relief Act of 2006.

I want to make a statement on behalf of the farm families of this country. When I came to Congress in the early 1990s, my farm families told me stories over and over again of their problems encouraging the next generation to farm the land that they farm. This is not a rich person's tax bill. This is a reasonable compromise.

Comment: he is so, full of it.

Four nays

(D-MI-14)

Mr. Conyers. Mr. Speaker, the House of Representatives is known as the "People's House." Instead of taking up legislation that will improve the lives of a wide range of people, we are debating a tax break that will benefit a measly 7,500 Americans, or in other words, only the super-rich.

(D-CT-1)

Mr. Larson of Connecticut. Mr. Speaker, I am disappointed in the Republican leadership and their priorities in this House. Instead of moving forward with the minimum wage increase that was approved last week in the House Appropriations Committee, the Republican Majority places yet another irresponsible estate tax cut bill on the floor.

(D-NY-17)

Mr. Engel. Mr. Speaker, as Ronald Reagan used to say—there you go again!

The Republicans would like us to believe that they are fiscal conservatives, but they are borrowing and spending like drunken sailors, abandoning all fiscal discipline.

As a result, we are leaving our children and grandchildren with mountains of debt for years to come. Of the millions of American families, this bill will allow 830 super rich families get a $16 million tax break—what a disgrace!

(D-CA-8)

Ms. Pelosi. Mr. Speaker, today the House is considering the ultimate values debate. The question before us today is, Do we want to cut taxes for the ultra-superrich, or, instead, do we first want to give hardworking Americans a raise?

Do we want to live in an aristocracy, or do we want to live in a democracy?

Do we want to perpetuate wealth or reward work?

The estate tax is central to our democracy. It is rooted in our commitment to create a strong and vibrant middle class and to give every American the opportunity to achieve the American Dream.

The bill passed by a vote of 257 to 156 in the House. I am shocked by how many congressmen are mentally retarded. The bill was placed on the Senate Legislative Calendar.

I think the people have forgotten the lesson of the "roaring twenties." It was an era when our country prospered tremendously—like the boon of the nineties: the Revenue Act of 1926, signed by Calvin Coolidge, reduced the federal income and inheritances, dramatically. Most of the profit went to the top—and there was an imbalance of wealth. The workers had little money to buy goods and services. This was one of the main causes that led to the Great Depression. So, the estate-death (or inheritance) tax—makes economic sense, in that, it is a just source of government revenue—and corrects wealth maldistribution.

Andrew Mellon, Coolidge's Secretary of the Treasury, the main force behind these tax cuts—was himself, one of the wealthiest men in the United States.

The strong economy that Bush's claims is the result of the tax cuts of the rich—is sustained by borrowing from foreign countries to pay for federal government expenses and using the Social Security Trust Funds—as a piggy bank. Other factors: sustaining this economy: (dangerously) high consumer credit card spending—and a large work force—making the minimum wage.

And the bad thing about a plutocracy—it will ignore public opinion or the truth—and do what it wants—anyway. They put self-gain—before the common good.

Critics of the Bush tax cuts

Ex-president Bill Clinton says: "Tax cuts are always popular, but about half of these tax cuts since 2001 have gone to people in my income group, the top 1 percent, I've gotten four tax cuts."

Robert Freeman—calls the Bush tax cuts: "a form of national insanity".

Senator Minority Leader Tom Daschle: calls Bush's tax cut: "obscene."

Senator Feingold said: Bush's economic stimulus plan is "entirely fiscally, Irresponsible."

Money guru Jan Bryant Quinn: called the $1.35 trillion tax cut signed by the President Bush in 2001: "a contemptible piece of consumer fraud."

Senator Kennedy: "Taking advantage of the suffering of millions of out-of-work Americans, the Bush administration is using the recession to justify major new tax breaks for the wealthy."

Rep. John Lewis, D-Ga., said: "We are failing the American people. This is not progress, this is greed. And it is disgraceful."

Robert McIntyre, Director of CTJ, said: "It would be nice to believe that after this latest defeat, the Congressional leadership will focus on solving our nation's real problem with the same zeal they're devoted to gutting the estate tax. Realistically, however, that's about as likely as pigs flying."

And the reason why polls—showed the majority of American people favoring the repeal of the estate state—quoted by congressmen and senators: it is because of un-enlightenment and a PR campaign funded by the super-wealthy—branding it the Death Tax and spreading misinformation (falsehoods).

FairEconomy.org—announced: April6, 2006: **Public Citizen and United for a Fair Economy Expose Stealth Campaign of Super-Wealthy to Repeal Federal Estate Tax.** The article states:

"In a massive public relations campaign, the families have also misled the country by giving the mistaken impression that the estate tax affects most Americans. In particular, they have used small businesses and family farms as poster children for repeal, saying that the estate tax destroys both of these groups. But just more than one-fourth of one percent of all estates will owe any estate taxes in 2006. And the American Farm Bureau, a member of the anti-estate tax coalition, was unable when asked by *The New York Times* to cite a single example of a family being forced to sell its farm because of estate tax liability."

Joan Claybrook, president of Public Citizen, says: "This report exposes one of the biggest con jobs in recent history. This long-running, secretive campaign funded by some of the country's wealthiest families has relied on deception to bamboozle the public not only about who must pay the estate tax, but about how repealing it will affect the country."

Floyd Norris reported in the *New York Times:* "In 2004, the latest year for which data are available, just 736 tax returns were filed for estates worth $20 million or more, and only 520 of them paid any estate tax at all." That is another problem, which needs fixing (tax loopholes). Tax reform should be Bush's top priority: not HR 8—repeal of the estate tax.

It is easy to learn how the estate tax is avoided—by looking at these returns. But, recently, the IRS announced, that it was drastically reducing the staff that audits the richest Americans.

The estate tax is an America (or good) principle: what makes it fair—or unfair: the rules, rates and brackets.

The following chart—gives a hawk's eye view of the creeping dismantle-ment—of the American estate tax—by plutocrats: the ultimate goal—(perma-nent) repeal.

THE ESTATE AND GIFT TAX TABLE

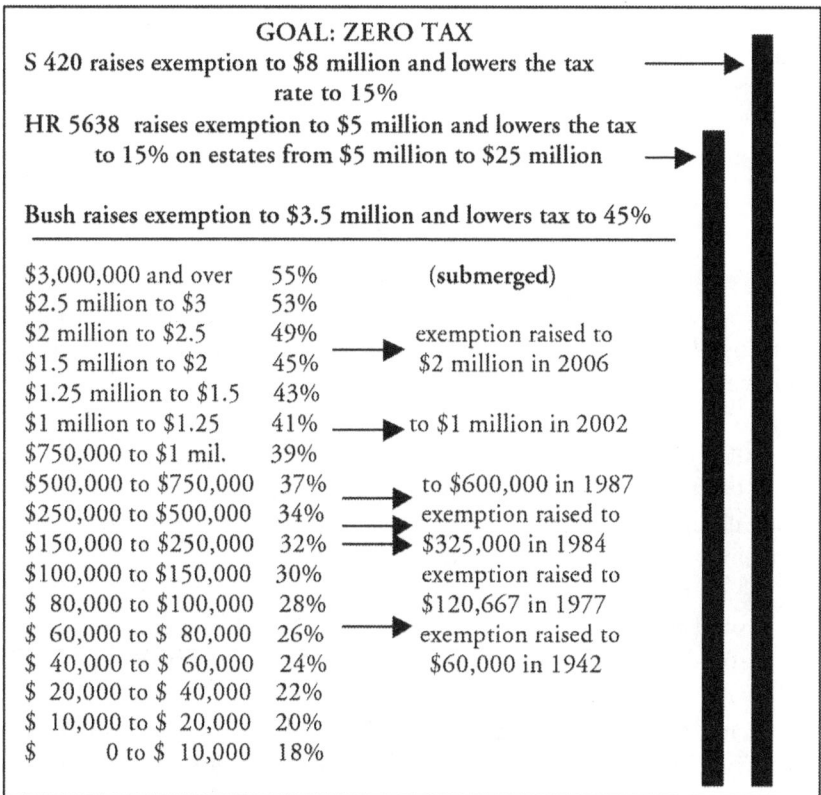

GOAL: ZERO TAX

S 420 raises exemption to $8 million and lowers the tax rate to 15%

HR 5638 raises exemption to $5 million and lowers the tax to 15% on estates from $5 million to $25 million

Bush raises exemption to $3.5 million and lowers tax to 45%

$3,000,000 and over	55%	(submerged)
$2.5 million to $3	53%	
$2 million to $2.5	49%	exemption raised to
$1.5 million to $2	45%	$2 million in 2006
$1.25 million to $1.5	43%	
$1 million to $1.25	41%	to $1 million in 2002
$750,000 to $1 mil.	39%	
$500,000 to $750,000	37%	to $600,000 in 1987
$250,000 to $500,000	34%	exemption raised to
$150,000 to $250,000	32%	$325,000 in 1984
$100,000 to $150,000	30%	exemption raised to
$ 80,000 to $100,000	28%	$120,667 in 1977
$ 60,000 to $ 80,000	26%	exemption raised to
$ 40,000 to $ 60,000	24%	$60,000 in 1942
$ 20,000 to $ 40,000	22%	
$ 10,000 to $ 20,000	20%	
$ 0 to $ 10,000	18%	

In 1976, the percentage of estates subject to the estate tax: 7.65%, after the Reagan and Bush increases in the exemption: it has dropped to 0.5 percent—and the top tax rate from 77 percent to the present 46 percent.

By clobbering the estate tax, "we are laying the groundwork" for a return to the sort of hereditary superrich and the class structure of the early 20th century portrayed in the movie "Titanic," says Sam Pizzigati, editor of Too Much.

There are three main ways of reducing the estate tax: increase exemption, lower the tax rate, and increase the lifetime gift credit allowance. Then, there are the rules, such as: marital deductions, generation-skipping, classification of people, such as: citizens and non-citizens, the way the tax code treats annuities, partnerships, trusts, charitable donations, etc.

Contradiction

The estate and gift are taxed the same in the table. But, there is a contradiction here.

An inheritance—is like a gift after death.

A gift—is like an inheritance during life.

Why, repeal the tax on the gift after death—and not the gift during life! HR 8—does that. That is a contradiction. The repeal of the estate tax for the year 2010—does the same thing. It continues to tax gifts made during life.

FRAUD

Also, I would like to point out: HR-8—contains an element of fraud. The estate tax—allows for a step-up tax basis (i.e., of evaluating assets). It exempts capital gains of $3 million for a surviving spouse and another $1.3 million for surviving heirs. The reason for this—so, heirs would not be double taxed for the estate and capital gains tax. Losing this exemption troubled some members of congress. In the debate—Hulshof (R)—assured them: the bill—allows for their retention. For which there is no legitimate bases—because, the estate tax would have been eliminated. To include this benefit—or exemption in the repeal—to induce members of congress to pass it—is trickery or fraud.

One thing I do agree with Bush: the tax code should be made simple; so, he can understand it. He has been misleading people—calling it the Death Tax.

The estate tax was 77 percent during World War II, the Korean War, and Vietnam War. Those that die in combat give 100 percent for the common good. Those that come home with severe brain trauma, missing an eye, or amputees, give up to 75 percent. Now, we are in war in Iraq and Afghanistan and Bush wants to repeal the estate tax on the wealthiest Americans, return zero to the common good. But, he has no problem sending men into harms way to protect the estates of the super-rich.

Bush, also, slashed Veteran's benefits in the 2004 Federal Budget nearly $30 billion to make up for the lost revenue from the 2001 and 2003 tax cuts on the rich.

Donald Rumsfeld, Secretary of Defense, will save an estimated $32 to $101 million from the repeal of the Death Tax. I wonder what his position is on this issue.

He is a member of Bush's cabinet.

Put your answer in the blank space_____ the troops want to know.

Here is how **Congressman Sherman** thinks: "We require the men and women in uniform to risk the ultimate sacrifice; and from our richest families, we say zero sacrifice under the estate tax. Shame."

CHAPTER 6

SUGGESTIONS

Where wealth accrues honorably, the people are always the silent partners.
—Andrew Carnegie

The term: Death Tax is misleading (or incomplete). It sounds like a tax on death.

The term: Estate Tax is misleading (or incomplete). It sounds like a tax on your estate: land, house, stocks, etc.

Both, however, are identical.

These are two-halves of the same tax: that need to be combined—to understand.

First of all, do we agree: the income and inheritance are two different taxes:

One: is a tax on income or wages paid by the individual during lifetime.

The other: is a tax on the inherited assets of a deceased person—paid by inheritors.

Therefore, the argument: that the Death-Estate-Tax is double taxation is not so. The death-estate tax is another form of the inheritance tax: pre-paid—by the estate executor—before distribution to heirs (or beneficiaries). It, just, sounds like double taxation; because, the decedent's estate—pays the inheritance tax for the heirs.

Unless, you think the income tax and inheritance tax—is double taxation.

I have not heard people call the inheritance tax—double taxation.

I have heard people call the Death tax—double taxation. But, they are the same.

Gasoline is triple-taxed—so what!

What better place to look for revenues—than, where there is a surplus—that is the estate of the deceased, who has accumulated large fortunes from investments and natural resource profits, much of which, has never been taxed—or lightly taxed. It is more fair—than, taxing the wages of the living poor and middle class—to pay for government expenses. When, FDR raised the estate tax in 1932—it was called the Revenue Act—not the Death Tax.

The progressive inheritance tax is fair—because, the greater the wealth—the more people it took—to achieve it.

A strong and fair inheritance—or estate tax is needed to solve America's financial crisis and reduce the disparity between the rich and poor in the next decade and beyond.

The problem with the present US estate tax: the personal exemption has been repeatedly raised to a very high level—to protect family farms and businesses from being destroyed—as property pass from one generation to the next—in the event of death. But, what happens: it lets pass assets up to the level—of $2 million per person (double for married couples) in 2006—to the next generation—tax free: that are not related to family farms or business: such as, stocks and bonds, real estate, etc.

The different between the inheritance tax and the estate tax—or so-called Death Tax is this:

The estate tax—imposes a tax on the assets left behind by the decedent—before distribution to inheritors.

The inheritance tax—imposes a tax on the assets of the decedent—after distribution to inheritors. They are mixed twins.

But, because, the personal exemption of the Federal estate tax has been raised so high—it misses taxation of all other tangible and intangible assets under the personal exemption level, that has been repeatedly raised—that are non-family farms and businesses—related.

Mrs. Hutchison (R-TX) said: "In fact, American has the highest death tax in the world." This is a derogatory term for the inheritance tax, but the truth of the matter: it has the highest personal exemption of any nation in the world.

Back in 1969—during the Vietnam War—the tax rates were 3% to 77%, the exemption: $60,000, and 5.02 percent of the estates of the deceased were subject to the tax.

In 2006—we are fighting a war in Iraq and Afghanistan, and the tax rate is 46%, the exemption: $2 million, and only 0.5% of estates of the deceased are subject to the tax. That is a huge drop. The goal—of the pro-dynastic wealth group—the elimination of the estate tax.

People might think this is a good thing, but not, when they see the consequences: the deficits, the cuts in health, education, welfare, etc. and the increase—or enactment of other taxes—to compensate for the lost revenue.

Elimination of waste in the government is good, but not the basics needs of the people—when, there is opulence at the top: millionaires and billionaires.

The increase in the concentration of wealth at the top in the US is "stunning", says Edward Wolff, New York University expert on wealth.

These are the figures published by the Center on Budget and Policy Priorities: the share of capital income flowing to households in various income categories:

	TOP 5%	BOTTON 80%
1979:	57.9%	23.1%
2003:	73.2%	12.6%

Considering these figures: the Bush tax cuts are misplaced—and grossly unfair. The repeal of the Death Tax—is the most egregious—in principle. Look at it this way: the collection of the accumulated unpaid taxes of the deceased. It is more fair to collect them from the past generation, than dump them on future generations. That is just one, of many justifications.

The Resurrection

I believe the estate tax should be spread out on more people—at least—the top 5 percent. The problem with the present estate tax—it levies a tax on only 5 of 1,000 estates and that will decrease to 3 out of 1,000 estates in 2009. This trend—needs to be reversed.

To do this—effectively and fairly—you need reform. I would change the exemption, the rates and brackets—and divide assets into two types.

ESTATE TAX

1a. On non-family farm and business assets: I would exempt the first: $500,000 per person. Then, levy a 5% estate tax on $500,000 to $1 million, 10% from $1 million to $2 million, 15% from $2 million to $3.5 million, 20% from $3.5 million to $5.5 million, 25% from $5.5 million to $10 million: 30% from $10 million to $16 million, 35% on $16 million to $25 million, and 40% on $25 million and over. Assets evaluated at fair market value—less liabilities.

Optional
(i.e., inheritance tax)

1b. On non-family farm and business assets: I would exempt the first $150,000 (i.e., recipients) Then, levy a 5% inheritance tax on $150,000 to $300,000, 10% from $300,000 to $600,000, 15% on $600,000 to $1 million, 20% on $1 million to $2 million, 25% on $2 million to $4 million, 30% on $4 million to $8 million, 35% on $8 million to $16, and 40% over $16 million.

ESTATE TAX

2. On family farms and business assets—I would exempt the first $2 million—based on continued use (or operation) by siblings—or heirs. Then, I would levy a 5% estate tax on assets from $2 million to $3 million: 10% on $3 to $6 million, 15% on $6 million to $12 million, and 20% on $12 million and over. I would stick with Section 6166 of the tax code. Farms and business assets evaluated on carry over basis—less liabilities.*

These rates above—leaves room for states to impose a small inheritance or estate tax.

By repealing: the federal estate tax—that places a heavier burden: on labor—taxation. That is HR 8.

That is unfair, because inherited wealth is unearned income (i.e., by heirs) or gains from investment. Why—should it be exempt—if, labor, wages, or earned income is taxed.

The inheritance tax is the same principle as the tax on gifts, money awards, prizes, lottery winnings, gambling, etc.

Do people—or congressmen want to eliminate these taxes also—or just the estate tax: that, mostly, affects the super-rich.

Sen. Kohl said: "The arguments surrounding estate tax repeal are muddled, and I believe there are important clarifications to make."

I do not have a problem with the gift tax bracket-rates—as it is. They, just, don't fit estate taxation. The estate tax is a tax on bulk assets—after death, before distribution to individuals—or recipients. The gift tax is a tax on gifts made during life-time to individuals—or inter vivos.

The gift tax is more closely related to the inheritance tax—which is paid by the recipients.

---

* This is based on a report: the average farm household net worth ranging from small $576,400 to large $1.5 million.

The gift and inheritances are different; because, one is yearly and the other: life-time.

Gifts are more closely related to income, because of the yearly and individual nature.

Also, taxing the donor for gifts—above the tax-free level—instead of the donee—is backwards. The person, who receives the gift—or benefit—should pay the tax—in most cases. In a few cases, the donor—or a bilateral agreement.

Most gifts should be taxed according the gift tax table—or income. Either is alright. I would separate—gift-giving from the estate tax. The lifetime cumulative gift credit allowance—makes it unnecessarily complex.

There is no need for a lifetime accumulative exemption—when taxing the recipient for gifts.

The way the gift tax is configured now—no tax is paid—unless you exceed your accumulative lifetime exemption and the high exemption—like the estate tax, submerges the lower tax rate brackets. That scheme—would be abolished— by making the gift tax—a yearly event paid by the recipient. That is more fair and produces more revenue.

Emerson said: "For every benefit you receive, a tax is levied." That is a statement of principle. But, recipients of gifts and inheritances—the way the US Tax Code is structured: there is no tax levied. That is a violation of principle.

The government cannot operate on the principle of benefit: profit, income, wages—and no tax.

You cannot buy something and not pay—that is not a good economic principle. As they say: "There is no free lunch."

There are a few exceptions, such as: charity, gifts on special occasions, etc.

The way the present US tax code is designed: it exempts the donor from paying the gift tax by enacting two exemptions: annual per donee and life-time accumulative—and the donee or recipient lives on gifts tax free. The larger the gift exemptions: the more it obviates the estate tax.

Gift giving to avoid the estate tax—is only a problem; if, there is no gift tax— or the exemption is too high. The devaluation of estate by gift-giving, can better be solved by taxing the recipient up front, in the form of a gift tax, than taxing the giver later—or after death. That is in compliance with natural principle. Taxing (or penalizing) the giver is not. Not taxing the recipient: means he pays no taxes on income, and yet receives all the benefits of government. That is a violation of natural principle. It penalizes the giver and the recipient pays no tax on income. Therefore, taxing the recipient for gifts, serves a dual purpose: the government collects the estate tax from the recipient or transferee and the recipient pays taxes on income—or gifts. I would not tax small gifts; but the present exemption is too generous. It has been raised by politicians—to avoid both the gift and estate tax paid by the donor. Taxing the recipient—changes the psychology. There is no justification for a big exemption—since, the gift is gratuitous. Taxing the donor is based on the assumption: the gift is intended to avoid the estate tax: not a true gift. The big increase in the per donee annual exclusion has become a big tax-free capital transfer tunnel for the ultra-rich.

The estate should be a separate tax.

The way the united estate and gift tax is formulated now: IS A DOUBLE TAX-BREAK FOR THE SUPER-RICH. It avoids the income tax and lowers the estate tax.

The parents can give $24,000 per year to siblings tax-free and lower their estate tax—by gift-splitting.

The children of the poor: work for the minimum wage and earn $10,300 per year and are subject to the income tax. That strikes me as being unfair.

The standard deduction for wages: $5,150.

The standard exemption for gifts: $12,000.

Big tax-free gift exclusions: allows the children of the rich—to live tax free—based on taxes parents paid. In other words: two generations for the price of one.

The government is shortchanged—when the second generation lives off the taxes paid by the first.

Caution: I am not referring to the family unit.

I am referring to descendents of the superrich.

There are two parts to this—inter vivos and after death. I will explain—the second part later.

Besides, the per person gift, lifetime exclusion: there is a $2 million per person exemption from estate taxation—or $4 million for married couples—in 2006. That climbs to $7 million in 2009—that can be transferred to the next generation tax free—in addition to unlimited gift-giving (not over $12,000).

And there is a third—extension to the current estate tax: it is the GST—exemption. It is the transfer of assets to second generation (or grandchildren). That exemption is equal to the estate tax exemption—currently—$2 million per person.

And, if HR 5638 passes the Senate: in 2010: $5 million per person inter vivos gifts in excess of the per donee annual exclusion can be transferred to descendents free of the gift tax. And the recipients pay no gift or income tax. The estate tax exemption also would be raised to $5 million: meaning you can transfer that amount in assets after death—per person to the next generation: free of estate tax and the recipient pays no inheritance or income tax. However, over the limit inter vivos gifts reduces the estate tax exemption. However, each person can make unlimited tax-free annual gifts up to $12,000 per donee during life, which does not reduce either exemption—and the recipient pays no gift or income tax. And it gets worst, according to the Poterba-Weisbenner study, large estates over $10 billion—were made up of 56.4 percent untaxed capital gains. That means: heirs or lineal descendents of the super-rich, almost, get a free ride.

And it gets worse: HR 5638—repeals the sunset provision of the generation-skipping tax exemption of EGTRRA of 2001—and increases it to $5 million. That means: $5 million per person can be transferred to second generation descendents (or grandchildren): tax free—double for married couples: or a total of $20 million: plus unlimited tax free giving within the rules.

This $20 million—**plus inter vivos gifts**—is exempt from the gift tax, the estate tax, and the heir's (or recipient's) income tax. Not only the first generation (children); but, the second generation (grand children)—can live almost tax-free and not work and receive all government benefits. And fifty percent of that $20—million: plus—might have escaped capital gains taxation—or never taxed. These tax-breaks for the rich are present in the current law—or tax code. But, the Thomas proposal—is a threefold big increase: the estate tax exemption, the accumulative lifetime gift-tax exemption, and the GST exemption to $5 million per person. It is 75% to 80% as costly as full repeal—and creates a American aristocracy to boot—that does not need to work, does not pay tax on their millions of dollar of inherited wealth—and receives all the benefits of the government. These triple big estate tax exemptions in the Thomas proposal are incredibly unfair. They are so unfair—I doubt my own figures.

GST tax exemption is so high: $10 million for married couples: the tax is irrelevant. Instead of being a tax—on generation-skipping transfers—it is a tax exemption.

And it gets even worse: HR 5638 reduces the highest gift tax from the present rate of 46% to 20%.

This is a giant tax break for the rich. The problem with this design: the heirs of super-rich families—live tax-free on multi-million dollar gifts and inheritances. And, the workingman—pays the income tax on wages. This is an unfair tax code. For example, I give a tip to a waitress: that is taxable, I give a gift—gratuitously, it is not taxed. It does not make sense—to tax something you worked for, and not tax something you have not worked for. That is nature reversed.

More ever, the 15% and 20% is not a true capital gains tax rate—because of the exemptions. For example: on a $10 million estate, after the $5 million per person exemption, the true tax rate is 7.5%. For couples—the tax is zero. The capital gains tax has no exemptions. It gives the impression of a higher tax—than it is. It does not equate with the capital gains tax. The three-double exemptions has the effect of lowering and eliminating the tax.

And worst yet—and the public is unaware of these things! They don't understand the Tax Code.

HR 5638 is written in code—that is, so, that people can't understand it. Bill Thomas is the bill's chief strategist. He introduced it to the House—without explaining its contents. Before debate begins, there should be a question and answer period on the floor, not behind closed doors. The bill-maker should ask—Are there any questions—before proceeding. I don't believe—(some) congressmen understood it—by their inane remarks.

Here is what **Rep. Blunt** (R-MO) said: "As I listen to this debate, what we are really talking about today is do we want to let this inheritance tax go back to the level that it was in 2001, where every family farm, every small business that had accumulate value and assets of $600,000 would see 65 percent of the excess of that go to the Federal Government."

He should do his homework—before speaking on the House floor. First, what he says: we, either, pass HR 5638—or go back to 2001. That is not the case. There is another option—a different reform bill. His statement—is full of mistakes.

One—the exemption in 2001 was $675,000—not $600,000. But, in 2011—according to ABA—the exemption is $1.1 million: double for married couples. And, the top rate is 55% not 65%. And, it does apply—until the estate reaches an aggregate net value of $3 million: over $1 million starts at 41%.

Considering the **Deficit**: the 2011 estate-gift tax is far fairer than HR 5638.

HR 5638—is a morass of legalese. It conceals gigantic tax-breaks for the top—less than 1 percent. You cannot see it by looking at the text of the bill—it needs explanation.

The reunification of the gift tax and estate tax: results in three big tax exemption increases and at the same time drastically reduces the gift and estate tax. It is designed: to avoid the gift and estate tax up to $5 million per person and $10 million for married couples and even $20 million using GST. The problem with HR 5638—it is good for the rich, but, cheats the commonwealth.

I have read summaries, but they don't address the gift tax—meta-big cuts. The gift tax table has been discarded and replaced with the capital gains tax. That is like putting square blocks in round holes: they don't fit. This is the work of a madman. Bill Thomas, the sponsor of the bill, is working on behalf of the GOP plutocracy. He is not representing the people. And, if, I understand this correctly, there is no tax on gifts until the accumulative lifetime total exceeds $5 million (or $10 million for couples)—and that tax will be the same as the capital gains tax.

The present lowest gift tax is 41%—it applies on gifts from $1 million to $1.25 million and the highest gift tax is 46% on gifts over $2 million. That is somewhat bad.

But, under HR 5638—the lowest gift tax is 15% and it applies on gifts from $5 million to $25 million and the highest 20% on gifts of over $25 million. This is a whopping big tax cut for the super wealthy—that don't need tax relief. The big-bad thing—the government is shortchanged.

The horrific thing: the House passed this tax bill without the people knowing its contents.

It not only should be explained to the congress—but, also the people. This bill constitutes legal stealing. It erodes the tax base and increases the tax burden on the less able to pay. The superrich receives the most benefit from national defense and homeland security. The top 20% of households owns 84.4% of the nation's wealth (2001).

This chart shows the gradual eradication of the gift tax—enacted to prevent the avoidance of the estate tax.

Year	top tax rate	annual exclusion	lifetime exempt.
1924	40%	$500	$50,000 (**annual**)
1942	77%	$3,000	$30,000
1984	55%	$10,000	$325,000
2006	46%	$12,000	$1 million
HR 5638			
2010	20%	? $12,000 (indexed)	$5 million

Now, combined with the reductions in the estate tax, we are back to a perpetual American aristocracy—inherited wealth and power—almost.

The recipient of a $1 million gift—pays no taxes: he pays no taxes on $5 million—or $10 million. However, on earned income over $325,000: the tax is 35 percent. That is not right. The tax on gifts is only 15% after it exceeds $5 million under the Thomas proposal. That is far lower than income tax on income from wages from $29,701 to $71,550, which is 25%.

The Tax Code is supposed to be fair.

It is a mismatch—to unite the gift tax with the estate tax. The estate tax of 15% on $5 million to $25 million and 20% over $25 million are not applicable to gift taxation. They are like a turkey sandwich and a whole roasted turkey.

Gifts should be treated—separately—and taxed on a year-to-year basis. The income or gift tax table should be used. This is more applicable to gift—taxation—than the capital gains tax. And the recipient should pay the tax—not the gift-giver. But, HR 5638 is designed, so neither pays.

By reversing principle: making the donor pay the gift tax: the recipient: pays no income tax: by raising the exemption, the donor pays no estate tax: by uniting the gift and estate tax, when you raise the exemption on the estate tax—you raise the exemption on the gift tax—and the donor pays to gift tax. It is a free ride for heirs or lineal descendents of the super-rich.

Howard Behar, former president of Starbuck International, said: "Passing on unlimited inheritances is not only bad for our children; it is also unhealthy for a democracy to tolerate concentrations of hereditary wealth and power. It is more important to give our kids education opportunities and encourage them to make their own way in the world of work. I have a moral responsibility to all children in our society, not just my own, to ensure access to quality education."

IMPORTANT CHANGES IN THE GIFT TAX

There are two parts to the gift-tax—other than rates and brackets.

- The annual per donee exclusion.
- The accumulative lifetime exemption.

The 1924 two gift tax exclusions were $500 per donee, per year, and the annual exclusion was $50,000 per donor. Excesses were paid on an annual bases. That was repealed and changed in 1932: the annual exclusion—became lifetime accumulative. That is the first big change.

Both of these have been sharply increased, since, 1976: good for the super-rich—bad for government tax revenues (or commonwealth).

In 1976: the lifetime accumulative gift tax exemption was: $30,000: above that level triggers the gift tax. Today, it is $1 million—a 3,333 percent increase.

The third big change: Reagan increased the annual exclusion per donee—from $3,000 to $10,000. That opened the floodgate to tax-free gift giving: that defeats or by-passes the estate tax—and gives lineal descendents—a free ride.

For example, based on the current law (2006): $24,000 gifts by married couples can be made to two children and four grandchildren for twenty year: totaling $2,880,000 tax-free. This does not cut into lifetime gift or estate exemptions.

That equals: $480,000 per recipient.

There are two principles involved here: good and bad.

Good: taxing wages or income. That is fair. That person pays for government services and benefits.

Bad: not taxing income from gifts and inheritances: that is unfair. That person does not pay for government services and benefits. That is a free ride (no work required).

That is bad enough; but HR 5635—increases the lifetime gift and estate exemption to $5 million per person—and lowers the tax rate: lower than wages.

Plus—unlimited untaxed gifts—up to $12,000 per year, per person (during life), which do not reduce lifetime accumulative gift and after-death estate tax exemptions.

The bill—creates a perpetual American Aristocracy: inherited wealth and power. It is close to full repeal.

The Chairman of the Ways and Means Committee—is suppose to devise a tax strategy to generate enough revenue for needed government expenses: the war in Iraq, domestic needs, reduce the deficit, etc. Bill Thomas has devised a tax plan to give the super-rich big tax breaks. For this, his party will support him and the mass media for reelection. Senator Daschle—who opposed Death Tax repeal—was unseated—by a vicious ad campaign. That is the power of a plutocracy. They have been able to convince people, that the Death Tax is bad.

Comparisons: $10 million estate	REVENUE BOX
Thomas: exemption: $5 million --------tax rate 15%	$750,000
Bush 2010 tax rate 0%	$ 0
2011 tax: exemption: $1 million ------tax rate 55%	$5.22 million
My Plan: exemption: $500,000 --------tax rate 30%	$2.85 million

You would think—US congressmen would be better informed. This save the family farm and small business argument—is so, in genuine. Most—could be exempted: by raising the Qualified Family Owned Business tax exemption to $2 million (or higher). Several proposals by Dorgan, Dayton, and others—tried to do this—or exempt family farms and business from the estate tax. These proposals or amendments were blocked in the congress. The Bush-GOP controlled Congress wanted the estate tax, which they call the Death Tax, phased out on the richest Americans—and repealed; i.e., EGTRRA (2001).

HR 8—is permanent repeal.

The Bush reductions of the Death Tax—increases the Birth Tax—each person's share of the deficit. And, that is wrong: the transfer of the debt to the next generation.

You could say: those that died—owed taxes and the rich more than the poor. The deficit is proof of under taxation. And here is, partially, why: the top 5 percent of Americans benefited the most, when Reagan dropped the income tax from 70% to 33%: their fortunes soared, and so, did the deficit: from $914 billion in 1980 to $3.1 trillion in 1990. So, you can say: the estate tax, in one sense, is the collection of unpaid taxes. Another justification: excessive compensation at the top, and under compensation at the bottom: sweat shops, etc.

Bush has acerbated the problem by cutting taxes, mostly at top—and increasing the Federal Deficit. Instead, of increasing the estate tax, to collect unpaid taxes, he has reduced the top rate and increased the exemption.

In 2010—the richest Americans—pay no estate tax. And the US deficit, at the present rate of growth, will reach $10 trillion by then, unless changes are made.

Mr. Bishop of Georgia—states (in the congressional records): the death tax should be eliminated to return to the American people and their progeny the hard-earned fruits of their labor. This sounds good. But, very few people make enough money by hard labor to become subject to the estate tax: it is fortunes made by the labors of others, business profits, capital gains from investments, and sometimes: avoiding taxation using accounting schemes and tax loopholes. Donald Trump did not become a billionaire by hard work. His tax returns will tell the truth.

But, the main debate here—is not the inequities of the present estate tax and the further multi-million dollar reductions of the Thomas proposal, but its total repeal.

Bush claims—repealing the estate tax—is "a matter of fairness". He said: "The death tax results in the double taxation of many family assets while hurting the source of most new jobs in this country—America's small business and farms." The problem with this statement: small business and farms—to not meet the threshold for estate taxation.

Bush has climbed on to the same bandwagon as the rest of the Republican plutocrats: repeal the estate tax to save small farms and family businesses—which has little substance; when, it is their own multi-million dollar fortunes—they are trying to save or transfer to heirs or lineal descendents 100% tax-free: some of it unethical and untaxed gains. But, they don't mind taxing hobbies, unemployment compensation, commissions, bonuses, etc.

Taxing things people worked for is fair.

But, taxing things people have not worked for—such as gifts and inheritances to recipients, that is unfair according to Bush and some members of congress. He is off-his-rocker.

Calling the estate tax—double taxation—is not a good argument, in the sense—estates of the deceased—have already been taxed: in the form of the income tax, etc.—for this reason. It is like the sales tax you pay on a new car—when sold, the new owner pays the sales tax again. The taxes your parents paid on income are for government services received during their lifetime, such as: homeland security, education, rebuilding of infrastructure, the armed services, etc. They terminate, when that person dies—they do not apply to the next generation. It is wrong—to think: you can inherit large sums of money, pay no inheritance tax, and receive all the benefits of the government, bases on the taxes your parents paid. Without the estate (or inheritance) tax: you create a two classes:

- The rich, that receive tax free inheritances and don't need to work, and receive all the benefits of government.

- The poor,* who don't receive inherited wealth, work for a living, and pay taxes on income for government services.

Heiress Leona Helmsley said: "Did you know that, only the little people pay taxes." True, some rich pay taxes, but some don't or too little. This is an unfair economic and political system. It is what Thomas Paine condemned: hereditary wealth and power. It did not work in France, Germany, Hungary, Austria, Russia, England, etc. for a number of reasons, such as: bad government, peasant revolts, incompetence, outdated, etc. And, the Abramoff-scandal exposes the sinister plot to put and keep in power—a GOP plutocracy.

Their top priority: KILL THE DEATH TAX.

What, President George W. Bush, the head of the GOP, is saying—in essence—the inheritance tax, which he calls—the "Death Tax"—is unfair and should be repealed, and heirs should live tax-free on the wealth earned and taxes paid by their parents—or grand parents, which is not only Anti-American—but, unfair, crazy, and illogical. He is a hardcore plutocrat—similar to George III. Senator Kennedy says: "It would be terribly unfair to tax work while giving inherited wealth a free ride"

Bush needs to go back to school!

Ralph Nader said: "The role of the inheritance tax is to counterbalance, modestly, the ability of the very rich and superrich to create family dynasties in which members by virtue of birth and birth alone have insuperable economic advantages over the rest of the society."

Before the debate ended in the House over HR 8, the permanent repeal of the estate tax, Congressman Kevin asked to extend his remarks. Here is what he said: "Mr. Speaker, in a few words, this is fiscal madness. It is a death wish on part of some of my colleagues about fiscal responsibility. What my colleagues are burying is fiscal responsibility."

And he added: "I hope, once again, the Senate will come to our rescue."

In the words of Senator Obama: "There is no economic justification for repealing the estate tax and certainly no moral justification. This is politics pure and simple."

Therefore, after examining the facts and the arguments on both sides, I have concluded: both the income and inheritance (or estate) tax are fair and needed to

---

* **The poor here: means workers and the middle class.**

bear the cost of government services and benefits and redistributes the accumulated wealth of the decedent—fairly, between heirs and the common good.

◻ The 2-type-asset-progressive tax would satisfy the critics: that argue the estate tax destroys family farms and business—and kills jobs.

◻ And, the 2-type-asset-progressive tax would satisfy critics of the estate tax repeal: that argue it is a needed source of government revenue—and serves to equitably redistribute accumulated wealth, when death occurs, and prevents the formation of an increasing powerful super-rich class—that destroys a democracy.

A plutocracy controls the government—not the people.

The rich get richer using capital-leverage-investing. Then, that is transferred to the next generation—and that grows again and soon, they owe nearly all the country's wealth (capital)—without the imposition of progressive taxation. Nobody—is advocating—repealing—this process, which is inherit in man; i.e., the strong force—or self-gain.

But, the strong force—should not obliterate the weak force: the good of others. The repeal of the estate tax—which the anti-estate tax forces—label the "Death Tax"—is America's form of the inheritance tax: that redistributes a percentage of the decedent's accumulated wealth—to the common good. Supporters of HR 8—want that principle repealed. Because of the growing number of more wealthy people: the estate tax—as a source of revenue—is becoming more needed. The second reason: the growing number of people that are becoming poorer. The bottom 40% of households owns less than 1% of the wealth (2001) less than 1983. The reduction or repeal of the estate tax would make matters worst: the rich richer and the poor poorer. Estate tax reform—would help!

The right balance—is a law of nature.

William H. Gates Sr.* said: "If we abolish the state's inheritance tax we stop the opportunity recycling program. We allow the common wealth to stop flowing and concentrate it in the hands of a few. And worse, we slow the investments in opportunity that aim to provided every young person a chance, whether they were born in South Seattle or Mercer Island."

The inheritance (or estate) tax is not only a state and federal principle, but worldwide.

---

* William H. Gates Sr. is a resident of Seattle. He is co-author with Chuck Collins of "Wealth and Our Commonwealth: Why America should Tax Accumulated Fortunes."

Here are some examples of the inheritance tax from other industrial nations.

England: 1 USD = 0.5254476 GBP

One rate: 40% £ 285,000 and over

Germany: 1 USD = 0. 780719 EUR

		Class I	Class II	Class II
Up to	52,000	7%	12%	!7%
	256,000	11%	17%	23%
	5,113,000	19%	27%	35%
	12,783,000	23%	32%	41%
	25,565,000	27%	37%	47%
over	25,565,000	30%	40%	50%

France: 1 USD = 0. 780719 EUR

6%	up to 7,600
10%	7,600 to 16,000
15%	16,001 to 30,000
20%	30,001 to 850,000
30%	850,001 to 1,700,000
40%	over 1,700,000

Japan   1 USD = 117.346   JPY

10%	8 million yen or less
15%	16 million yen or less
20%	30 million yen or less
25%	50 million yen or less
30%	100 million yen or less
40%	200 million yen or less
50%	400 million yen or less
60%	2 billion yen or less
70%	over 2 billion or less

Taiwan—estate tax is progressive. It is levied on the properties own by the decedent: stating at 2% up to NT $300,000 and rising to 60% for the incremental amounts of NT $160,000,000 or more.

Spain   1 USD = 0.780719 EUR

     16 Brackets

Lowest: 0 up to 7,993.46   7.65%
Highest: over 797,555.08   34%

South Korea has a top rate of 50%. The first 200 million won of inheritance assets is exempt from taxation ($210,666)

USA ESTATE TAX

   46% over $2 million ------2006

• **Russia abolishes inheritance tax ranging from 5% to 40%.**

The noticeable—difference: the inheritance tax of these nations and the United States, except for England, they begin at a lower rate, and have many progressive tax-rate-brackets. One reason for this: the Congress raised the personal exemption—to protect family farms and businesses. But for people, who do not own farms or businesses: these rates and exemptions—are unjustified. In 1916—the exemption began at $50,000. It was raised to $60,000 in 1942—to $120,667 in 1977, to $225,000 in 1982—and it was raised in stages to $675,000 in 2000. Then, Bush came to office and rapidly raised the exemption in increments to $3.5 million from 2002 to 2009—and completely repealed it for one year in 2010—for no good reason. The super-rich are not in need of tax relief. It is a crippling of the inheritance tax—that erases the lower tax rates and brackets, and raises the estate tax exemption too high, and generates too little revenue, and excludes 99.5 percent of taxpayers. It is a screwed up, tax avoiding, phasing in and out, overlapping, amended, re-amended and revised, full of loopholes, vilified and nearly clobbered to death estate tax—**that needs reform (and understanding).**

End of debate

978-0-595-42189-3
0-595-42189-X

www.ingramcontent.com/pod-product-compliance
Lightning Source LLC
Chambersburg PA
CBHW021037180526
45163CB00005B/2159